JOHN SAXBEE

WAY**MARK**ERS

A route map
through Lent
to Easter

www.kevinmayhew.com

KM PUBLISHING

First published in Great Britain in 2013 by Kevin Mayhew Ltd
Buxhall, Stowmarket, Suffolk IP14 3BW
Tel: +44 (0) 1449 737978 Fax: +44 (0) 1449 737834
E-mail: info@kevinmayhew.com

www.kevinmayhew.com

ISBN 978 1 84867 678 7
Catalogue No. 1501418

Cover design by Justin Minns
© Images used under licence from Shutterstock Inc.
Edited by Linda Ottewell
Typeset by Richard Weaver

Printed and bound in Great Britain

Contents

About the author

John Saxbee retired as Bishop of Lincoln in 2011. Born in Bristol, he studied at Bristol and Durham Universities. His doctoral research was on the writings of Soren Kierkegaard. He was ordained in 1972 and held parochial posts in Plymouth before being appointed Director of Training for the Diocese of Exeter and Joint Director of the South West Ministry Training Course. He was Bishop and Archdeacon of Ludlow for eight years before translation to Lincoln in 2001. His publications include *Liberal Evangelism* (SPCK 1994) and *No Faith in Religion* (O Books 2009). He reviews books on religion and philosophy for various journals.

John has contributed to the following publications for Kevin Mayhew: *Faith Matters* (1501369), *Facing the Issues* (1501353) and *More Sermons on Difficult Subjects* (1501389).

Introduction

A wide consensus has emerged amongst New Testament scholars that Mark's Gospel was the first to be written – probably about thirty or forty years after Jesus' death. Although we do not know for sure the identity of the author, an early tradition links him to St Peter and to the John Mark who features in the Acts of the Apostles (see Acts 12). It would seem likely that Matthew and Luke knew Mark's Gospel, and drew on it themselves, even though they also had additional sources as well.

Mark's is the shortest of the four New Testament Gospels but it packs an awful lot into just sixteen chapters. It can be read comfortably at one sitting, and it might be a good idea to do that as we set out on our journey through Lent to Easter. Frankly, there is no better route map for this journey than the one Mark provides – and we might well feel that he is appropriately named as he provides wayMARKers along the way to keep us focused on Jesus our companion, and on the cross and resurrection to which his destiny is calling him.

Whilst a specific passage will be reproduced for each stage of our journey, it will be wise to have a Bible by you throughout as you may want to cross-reference to other passages from time to time.

A sort of mini-commentary on the chosen text will be provided together with opportunities for reflection at appropriate points along the way. If this journey is being made in a group, then the leader can guide members through the commentary and also use the reflection opportunities to stimulate discussion. Pointers to reflection are between [ ] in bold type.

The sections of the commentary entitled **By the way** throw additional light on the text, but can be omitted if time is short.

Note: The chosen text can simply be read through silently or out loud, but members of a group may enjoy using **The Dramatised Bible** or hearing the passage read online or from a recording.

Our seven stage schedule charts the route to be taken, and if you can familiarise yourself with the relevant text before each session that will be good.

At the beginning of each stage of the journey there will be an opportunity to prepare – perhaps with the help of some music and/or visual images. Resources will be provided to assist in reflection and prayer, including opening prayers and an incremental prayer which will have biddings added stage by stage, so that insights from earlier stages are not forgotten, and new insights are given prayerful expression.

People on a journey often carry a rucksack, and it is suggested that this metaphorical rucksack is filled with lessons learned, experiences shared and resolutions to take into the future. So towards the end of each stage a reminder will be given about the rucksack, and encouragement to think about what might be taken forward from one stage to the next.

One last observation before we get underway: a notable characteristic of Mark's Gospel is that it is written in what might be described as rather rough Greek. His style is often somewhat colloquial and from time to time Matthew and Luke see fit to polish it up a bit when they recycle his material. This has led some people to conclude that Mark was a simple soul with little theological sophistication. He seems to push the story on at a hectic pace (the Greek word *euthus* meaning 'straight away' or 'immediately' occurs more than forty times in Mark). When compared with the other Gospels, Mark appears to be more anxious to tell the story than to explain what it means. But this assessment runs the risk of missing out on Mark's theological purpose and the serious theological message he wishes to convey, even if we need to dig a little deeper to extract the nuggets of gold.

So welcome to the wonderful world of Mark – and as we journey towards Easter may we discover that there is more to Mark than meets the eye.

Stage one
Travelling light – but not alone
(Mark 1:1-20)

Opening prayers

Blessed Lord, you have caused all holy scriptures to be written for our learning: grant that we may so hear them, read, mark, learn, and inwardly digest them, that by patience and comfort of your holy Word, we may embrace and ever hold fast the blessed hope of everlasting life, which you have given us in our Saviour Jesus Christ. Amen.

God our creator, redeemer and sustainer of life, go with us on this journey through Lent so that, with you as our companion and guide, we find the way that leads to life and follow it to the end. This we ask in the name of him who died and was raised for us, Jesus Christ, our Lord. Amen.

Our Father . . .

Setting the scene

As we begin 'the beginning of the gospel about Jesus Christ, the Son of God' (Mark 1:1) it will help us to have a feel for Mark's opening narrative if a sequence of a dozen or so images can be projected onto a screen depicting desert and wilderness locations. These can be downloaded from the internet by typing 'Desert' or 'Wilderness' into the web search facility. Run the sequence for four or five minutes, perhaps with some appropriate music to create an atmosphere and assist meditation.

Bible reading
Mark 1:1-20

¹The beginning of the gospel about Jesus Christ, the Son of God.

²It is written in Isaiah the prophet:

> 'I will send my messenger ahead of you,
>   who will prepare your way' –
> ³'a voice of one calling in the desert,
>   "Prepare the way for the Lord,
>   make straight paths for him."'

⁴And so John came, baptising in the desert region and preaching a baptism of repentance for the forgiveness of sins. ⁵The whole Judean countryside and all the people of Jerusalem went out to him. Confessing their sins, they were baptised by him in the Jordan River. ⁶John wore clothing made of camel's hair, with a leather belt round his waist, and he ate locusts and wild honey. ⁷And this was his message: 'After me will come one more powerful than I, the thongs of whose sandals I am not worthy to stoop down and untie. ⁸I baptise you with water, but he will baptise you with the Holy Spirit.'

⁹At that time Jesus came from Nazareth in Galilee and was baptised by John in the Jordan. ¹⁰As Jesus was coming up out of the water, he saw heaven being torn open and the Spirit descending on him like a dove. ¹¹And a voice came from heaven: 'You are my Son, whom I love; with you I am well pleased.'

¹²At once the Spirit sent him out into the desert, ¹³and he was in the desert for forty days, being tempted by Satan. He was with the wild animals, and angels attended him.

[14]After John was put in prison, Jesus went into Galilee, proclaiming the good news of God. [15]'The time has come,' he said. 'The kingdom of God is near. Repent and believe the good news!'

[16]As Jesus walked beside the Sea of Galilee, he saw Simon and his brother Andrew casting a net into the lake, for they were fishermen. [17]'Come, follow me,' Jesus said, 'and I will make you fishers of men.' [18]At once they left their nets and followed him.

[19]When he had gone a little farther, he saw James son of Zebedee and his brother John in a boat, preparing their nets. [20]Without delay he called them, and they left their father Zebedee in the boat with the hired men and followed him.

[Reflect on personal experiences of deserts, moors and wilderness. What effect do they have on our feelings about nature, God, ourselves and other people?]

It is usual to experience in wilderness places something of the awesomeness of nature, but also its ability to make us feel very small, insignificant and fearful. God's awe-inspiring power and grandeur could be overwhelming, yet the desert is also the place where people have felt God to be very close and accessible.

That Mark begins his Gospel in the wilderness is theologically significant. The people would associate wilderness with Israel's exodus from Egypt. It was remembered as a time when God blessed them, but it was also associated with the rebellion of the chosen people against God's rule over their lives. The desert became associated with the coming of the Messiah who would be announced by a voice crying in the wilderness.

But it can also be the case that we begin to see ourselves and other people in a different light as the result of a desert experience. Stripped of our status and pretensions, we and they are reduced to an equal and common concern for the basics – what to eat, where to sleep and how to attend to our personal hygiene. You don't want to be weighed down with inessential things in such a challenging and hostile environment. It is where we learn to travel light and only have about us the things which really matter.

So Mark's Gospel opens with a voice crying in the wilderness, and it was only by going out to meet John the Baptist in the Judean desert that the people from the countryside of Judea and the city of Jerusalem could hear that voice. It is a voice which focuses on the things that really matter: getting right with God by confession of sins and forgiveness through baptism in preparation to meet the one for whom John prepares the way i.e. he who will baptise with the Holy Spirit.

Mark's message is clear: before you can really engage with 'Jesus Christ, the Son of God' there is somewhere you have to go (the wilderness), someone you have to meet (John the preacher of repentance) and something you have to hear (his call to a new way of life). So it is that in preparation to meet Christ at Christmas we set aside the season of Advent to meet with John in the wilderness, and in preparation to walk with Jesus the way of the cross we set aside the season of Lent. In this season we reacquaint ourselves with John and his message sounded anew 'in the wilderness of this world's temptations'.*

---

* From the Bishops' Charge to Priests in the Anglican Ordinal.

This is a serious and, some might say, severe way to begin a Gospel when gospel means 'good news'! But it was a process of preparation which Jesus took to heart when he was himself baptised by John in the Jordan, and submitted to forty days of rigorous testings and temptations. He learned to travel light on the journey ahead of him – and so must we.

[Reflect on how, for some people, travelling light through Lent means giving something up as a symbol of our need to focus on what really matters. What might 'travelling light' mean for you and your Church 'in the wilderness of this world's temptations'?]

So Mark sets the scene for what follows with the preaching of John the Baptist, the baptism of Jesus and his forty days of temptation in the wilderness. These thirteen verses do for Mark what the infancy narratives do for Matthew and Luke (chapters 1 and 2) and the Prologue does for John (1:1-14). They establish from the outset that Jesus is the expected Messiah, the Son of God, the Word made flesh. Mark the theologian sets out his stall in a clear, colourful and concise curtain-raiser.

Now, we may be called to travel light, but not to travel alone. When Jesus begins his own ministry, inspired by John and the gifting of the Holy Spirit, he is forthright in proclaiming his message: the time is now, the place is here, the message is this (see Mark 1:15). But he then sets about securing a band of followers to accompany him on this epic adventure (Mark 1:16-20).

By the way

- Note that the little points of detail in these verses e.g. the casting of the net in verse 16 and the preparation of the nets in verse 19 provide early indications that eye-witness testimony – whether Simon Peter's or someone else's – lies behind Mark's account.

- Note also that Old Testament references to 'fishing for men' are invariably to do with rounding people up to face God's judgement (see Jeremiah 16:16 and Amos 4:2). But here Mark flips the meaning over so that now, under the terms of the new covenant, people are to be 'caught' as a means to their salvation rather than damnation.

- Finally note that in the time of Jesus, rabbis did not choose followers – followers chose them by shopping around until they found the one who was most compelling, convincing or simply congenial. Jesus demonstrates his special brand of authority by calling followers to him rather than waiting for them to seek him out.*

How did he choose these particular disciples? Not, apparently, by using the methods with which we are most familiar.

[Reflect for a moment on what those methods are. Do interviews come to mind, or tests, or talent contests, or various processes of elimination, such as are used on TV reality shows where the winner is effectively the last one standing – and the winner takes all?]

---

* R. Burridge, *Imitating Jesus* (Eerdmans, 2007), pp. 46-50.

Jesus seems simply to have called the first men he set eyes upon as he walked beside the lake, and challenged them to leave their day jobs and follow him. True, the fact that he was by the lake meant that the men he met were likely to be fishermen **[and you might reflect on why that would matter to him]**. But nevertheless, he still seems to have made choices at random. **[Are there lessons we can learn from this? What might it say to us about ourselves as followers, and about all those others who are counted with us as Christians i.e. followers of the Way (Acts 9:2)?]**

Much has been made of whether or not those who call themselves Christians are entitled to do so, and throughout history tests have been applied to determine who is and who isn't a true follower. That is all right as far as it goes, given that any movement or organisation needs some clarity about who's in and who's out. But the calling by Jesus of his first disciples was apparently gratuitous and an act of grace rather than the outcome of a strictly constructed selection process. All are in equal need of God's grace and God's grace is equal to the needs of all. So the journey we begin now as followers together in the way of Christ is one to which we are called, not through any merit of our own, but by God's grace. For that we can give thanks in the words of that former slave trader turned convert to Christianity, John Newton:

Saviour, if of Zion's city
I through grace a member am,
let the world deride or pity,
I will glory in thy name.

Note that it is not so much a matter of inviting Jesus into our lives, but him inviting us into his. During Lent Jesus calls us to walk with him, and we will not walk alone.

For the rucksack

What from this first stage of our journey will you especially want to take with you as we journey on?

Incremental prayer

Jesus Christ, Companion and Guide, go with us on this journey into life;

help us to sit loose to this world's trappings and temptations, and to travel light.

Thank you for those who have gone before us, those who go with us, and those we will encounter on the way. In meeting with us may they meet with you.

Amen.

Stage two

Stormy weather

(Mark 4:35-41)

Opening prayers

Blessed Lord, you have caused all holy scriptures to be written for our learning: grant that we may so hear them, read, mark, learn, and inwardly digest them, that by patience and comfort of your holy Word, we may embrace and ever hold fast the blessed hope of everlasting life, which you have given us in our Saviour Jesus Christ. Amen.

God our creator, redeemer and sustainer of life, thank you for calling us to follow you.
As we make our way, may we be ever aware of your presence with us, especially in times of doubt and danger.
As Jesus calmed the storm, so may he calm our fears and keep us firm in faith and hope and love.
For his name's sake we ask it. Amen.

Our Father . . .

Setting the scene

Again, some visual images downloaded from the internet can help to set the tone for this stage of the journey. Just type 'storms at sea' or the names of specific seas and oceans (e.g. Lake of Galilee, Atlantic Ocean etc.) into the web-search facility and it should be able to access images without too much difficulty. Suitable music to help create an atmosphere and assist meditation might accompany the sequence of images – four or five minutes will be sufficient.

Following on from the call of the disciples, Jesus' ministry begins at a frantic pace. Mark's Gospel is noted for the way the story hurries along with accounts of miraculous healings, exorcisms, teaching sessions and various encounters – some friendly, some hostile – punctuated by times for prayer and some peace and quiet (Mark 1:21–4:34).

This was the peace and quiet Jesus was seeking when he took to the water with his disciples to get away from the crowd.

Bible reading
Mark 4:35-41

[35]That day when evening came, he said to his disciples, 'Let us go over to the other side.' [36]Leaving the crowd behind, they took him along, just as he was, in the boat. There were also other boats with him. [37]A furious squall came up, and the waves broke over the boat, so that it was nearly swamped. [38]Jesus was in the stern, sleeping on a cushion. The disciples woke him and said to him, 'Teacher, don't you care if we drown?'

[39]He got up, rebuked the wind and said to the waves, 'Quiet! Be still!' Then the wind died down and it was completely calm.

[40]He said to his disciples, 'Why are you so afraid? Do you still have no faith?'

[41]They were terrified and asked each other, 'Who is this? Even the wind and the waves obey him!'

'A furious squall blew up' (verse 37) – a sudden unexpected disturbance which can blow the best-laid plans off course. One of the most predictable things about the Christian life is that it is pretty unpredictable!

[You may want to reflect on ways in which unpredicted events blew your plans off course – for better or worse. God does indeed move in mysterious ways as most of us can testify. Perhaps we can think about the idea of 'retrospective providence' i.e. when we look back on things which have happened to us, including events which seemed to have blown our plans out of the water, we can see the hand of God at work. Someone once said: 'If you want to make God laugh, tell him your plans.' Well, our plans may not raise a laugh but they might cause God to smile as his plans turn out to be better than ours!]

The disciples are alarmed, which is somewhat ironic as they are the ones who know the lake so well, and are familiar with the storms which can erupt at a moment's notice and cause consternation amongst the uninitiated. So we can assume that this must have been more violent than usual, and that adds to the drama as the story unfolds.

However, Jesus sleeps on. We have noted the busy schedule he pursued in the days leading up to this point, and he is clearly exhausted. Of course, this contrast with the panic displayed by the disciples also adds to the drama. They rouse him with what, in the circumstances, is a crass accusation: 'Do you not care?' It was precisely on account of his care for God's people that Jesus came into the world and, as John 3:16 underlines, his concern was that they 'should not perish, but have eternal life'. Nonetheless, Jesus is roused and proceeds to calm the storm and so allay their fears.

Note that this is the first miracle Jesus performs which is not an act of healing or exorcism. That is significant, because in the world of Jesus' time healers were fairly familiar figures who plied what could be a lucrative trade. Jesus differed from them in important ways e.g. he didn't look for payment or public recognition (although he did think that a little thanks wouldn't go amiss, as in the story of the ten lepers (Luke 17:11-19).

So the phenomenon of itinerant healers was not uncommon. However, the same cannot be said for acts which miraculously intervened in the course of nature. These were assumed to belong to the realms of the gods in classical mythology or, in the case of e.g. Moses parting the Red Sea, to the kingdom of God. So when Mark attributes to Jesus a miracle which involves stilling waves and calming storms, he is significantly raising the stakes when it comes to Jesus' identity as Messiah and Son of God, because it is precisely this kind of power and authority over the natural world which defines divinity in the Hebrew scriptures (see Psalm 89:8, 9; Isaiah 51:9, 10). Throughout the first half of his Gospel Mark insists on Jesus' true identity being kept under wraps – what has been described as Mark's 'messianic secret' notwithstanding the opening verse and the voice from heaven at his baptism. Peter's confession at Caesarea Philippi (Mark 8:27-38) gains added effect precisely because of how Jesus' identity has been protected up to that point in his ministry. But there is no doubt that this nature miracle on the lake of Galilee was bound to raise questions in many minds about Jesus' identity – 'Who is this? Even the wind and the waves obey him!' (4:41).

But now let us delve a little deeper into this story by comparing the ways in which it is told by Matthew, Mark and Luke. We have already noted that Matthew and Luke were probably well acquainted with Mark's Gospel, and this is confirmed by the fact that they reproduced most of his narrative with often only relatively minor changes in style or vocabulary. But here is a case where one of them makes a change which is of real significance, and it is to do with the order of events.

Read Mark 4:35-41, then Luke 8:22-25 and then Matthew 8:23-27. Take particular note of the order in which things happen. Matthew introduces a variation which gives us pause for thought. **[Spot the difference!]** Luke follows Mark in describing how they launch out on to the lake, a storm blows up, Jesus sleeps, the disciples rouse him and challenge him about his care for them, Jesus calms the storm and then challenges them about their lack of faith. Finally, the amazement of all concerned is noted. Matthew subtly reverses two elements in this sequence and thereby adds another dimension to the overall meaning. Instead of chiding the disciples for their lack of faith after he has stilled the storm, Jesus confronts them even as the storm is still raging around them and causing them so much consternation. Perhaps Matthew has simply made a mistake in recycling Mark's account. But that is unlikely. We should assume that he intended this change and that he had a point to make.

[Reflect on what that point might be. If you put yourself into the place of the disciples, how might your reaction be affected by whether Jesus' challenge comes before or after the storm has been stilled? Perhaps we can reflect

that it might be thought obvious that faith should follow upon witnessing that kind of miracle, especially when you have feared for your life. So in that case Jesus' chiding of them is well justified – and they might feel a bit sheepish or guilty. But to have faith whilst the storm is still at its height is a tougher call, and Jesus' challenge acquires a corresponding sharpness but also a sense of reassurance. It is worth remembering that those for whom Matthew's Gospel was written may well have been undergoing persecution at the time and so this challenge to have faith even as the storm was raging around them would have had especial poignancy. And what of us? It is when the storms of life are threatening to overwhelm us that we particularly need to take note of what Matthew is teaching us through this small change to Mark's original.]

So we see here how Mark's original story, perhaps told by him in calmer times, provides the raw materials out of which Matthew is able to fashion something much more directly relevant to his readers.

By the way

Before we finish this stage of our journey we note that there was another incident on the lake, which Mark describes (6:45-52) and which Matthew elaborates in much the same way as the story of the stilling of the storm (Matthew 14:22-33). This is the story of Jesus walking on the water when, once again, the disciples are battling with stormy weather. They are afraid – both of the storm and of the apparition they see coming towards them – and Jesus is gently reassuring:

'Take courage! It is I. Don't be afraid' (Mark 6:50). But in Matthew's hands the story acquires a sharper edge as Peter rises to the challenge of trying himself to walk on the water towards Jesus. But his nerve fails him and, according to Jesus, so does his faith as Peter begins to sink beneath the waves. Jesus hauls him out and is pretty firm with him: 'You of little faith,' he said, 'why did you doubt?'(Matthew 14:31).

Peter sinks because he became distracted by the storm and took his eyes off Jesus who has called him to take these courageous steps. Once more we sense that Matthew has added details to Mark's story which serve to challenge but also comfort Christians when storms erupt around them – whether in the form of persecution or, more likely today, the unpredictable setbacks which threaten our well-being and can seriously test our faith and endurance.

[Perhaps take a straw poll to see which of these approaches to storm-tossed incidents on the lake – Mark's or Matthew's – speaks most directly into our situation today.]

For the rucksack

What from this stage of our journey will you especially want to take with you as we journey on?

Incremental prayer

Jesus Christ, Companion and Guide, go with us on this journey into life;
help us to sit loose to this world's trappings and temptations, and to travel light.

Thank you for those who have gone before us, those who go with us, and those we will encounter on the way. In meeting with us may they meet with you.

Make us unafraid to face troubled waters knowing you are our still centre at the height of the storm.
Strengthen our faith to trust in you even as the winds and waves threaten to overwhelm us – for you are the Lord of sea and sky.
Amen.

Stage three

Brief encounters

(Mark 5:21-43)

Opening prayers

Blessed Lord, you have caused all holy scriptures to be written for our learning: grant that we may so hear them, read, mark, learn, and inwardly digest them, that by patience and comfort of your holy Word, we may embrace and ever hold fast the blessed hope of everlasting life, which you have given us in our Saviour Jesus Christ. Amen.

God our creator, redeemer and sustainer of life, thank you for those who enrich our lives by their companionship and love. Help us to see you in all those we meet on our journey through life, and make us the channels of your generous love to those who feel vulnerable and alone.
Open your Word that we may discern your will, and open our hearts that we may live the life revealed to us in your Son, Jesus Christ, our Lord. Amen.

Our Father . . .

Setting the scene

If possible, play part of the second movement from Rachmaninoff's Second Piano Concerto. [**Do you recall the most famous film to feature this music?** *Brief Encounter* **is a poignant portrayal of a chance meeting which had**

far-reaching implications. Reflect on any such brief encounters which for you and others have proved to be particularly significant and memorable.]

Jesus must have had many brief encounters with people on his travels, and some have been included in Mark's Gospel. The two described in this passage are particularly memorable:

Bible reading
Mark 5:21-43

²¹When Jesus had again crossed over by boat to the other side of the lake, a large crowd gathered round him while he was by the lake. ²²Then one of the synagogue rulers, named Jairus, came there. Seeing Jesus, he fell at his feet ²³and pleaded earnestly with him, 'My little daughter is dying. Please come and put your hands on her so that she will be healed and live.' ²⁴So Jesus went with him.

A large crowd followed and pressed around him. ²⁵And a woman was there who had been subject to bleeding for twelve years. ²⁶She had suffered a great deal under the care of many doctors and had spent all she had, yet instead of getting better she grew worse. ²⁷When she heard about Jesus, she came up behind him in the crowd and touched his cloak, ²⁸because she thought, 'If I just touch his clothes, I will be healed.' ²⁹Immediately her bleeding stopped and she felt in her body that she was freed from her suffering.

³⁰At once Jesus realised that power had gone out from him. He turned around in the crowd and asked, 'Who touched my clothes?'

³¹'You see the people crowding against you,' his disciples answered, 'and yet you can ask, "Who touched me?"'

³²But Jesus kept looking around to see who had done it. ³³Then the woman, knowing what had happened to her, came and fell at his feet and, trembling with fear, told him the whole truth. ³⁴He said to her, 'Daughter, your faith has healed you. Go in peace and be freed from your suffering.'

³⁵While Jesus was still speaking, some men came from the house of Jairus, the synagogue ruler. 'Your daughter is dead,' they said. 'Why bother the teacher any more?'

³⁶Ignoring what they said, Jesus told the synagogue ruler, 'Don't be afraid; just believe.'

³⁷He did not let anyone follow him except Peter, James and John the brother of James. ³⁸When they came to the home of the synagogue ruler, Jesus saw a commotion, with people crying and wailing loudly. ³⁹He went in and said to them, 'Why all this commotion and wailing? The child is not dead but asleep.' ⁴⁰But they laughed at him.

After he put them all out, he took the child's father and mother and the disciples who were with him, and went in where the child was. ⁴¹He took her by the hand and said to her, *'Talitha koum!'* (which means, 'Little girl, I say to you, get up!'). ⁴²Immediately the girl stood up and walked around (she was twelve years old). At this they were completely astonished. ⁴³He gave strict orders not to let anyone know about this, and told them to give her something to eat.

Apart from the twelve disciples he calls to follow him, and the ever-present scribes and Pharisees, most of the people Jesus encounters do not feature again in the gospel story.

There was Peter's mother-in-law (1:29-31); the leper who Jesus healed (1:40-45); a paralysed man and his four friends (2:1-12); the man with the withered arm (3:1-6); a man called Legion possessed of an evil spirit (5:1-20).

Now we come to Jairus, his daughter, and the woman with haemorrhages – memorable encounters with so much to teach us. It really matters that it is through the medium of these sorts of stories that the Markan Jesus teaches us about how to live according to the values of the kingdom of God, especially when it comes to how we treat people banished to the margins of society. Matthew and Luke include in their Gospels many chapters devoted to the moral teaching of Jesus. But for Mark it is more a matter of learning by example. We learn about how to live a righteous life by studying how a righteous life is lived. Jesus lived such a life, and it is from his daily encounters with a whole range of different people that we learn the lessons which matter most to us who seek to be followers of the Way.

Two lessons stand out from across the kaleidoscopic range of these encounters.

First of all, no two of them are the same. Jesus doesn't have a predetermined and carefully honed policy when it comes to how he responds to those he encounters. Each of them is different, and the circumstances in which they find themselves are never identical. So he relates to them as unique individuals in the immediacy of their current situation. He applies spittle to the eyes of a blind man because something tactile is important to someone who cannot see (8:22-26); and he uses a word which can be easily lip-read in restoring hearing to a deaf man (7:31-37).

But, as we shall see, it is not only by the use of physical gestures that Jesus affirms each person's individuality. Emotional and spiritual contact matters as well. All too often our ethical stances as Christians appear to be sweeping generalisations when what is necessary – and most Christ-like – is a care and concern for this single individual in the here and now of their lives and ours. Of course the ethical teaching of Jesus in, for example, the Sermon on the Mount, is important but Mark also wants us to notice and imitate how Jesus applied that teaching because what we do as well as what we say defines us as disciples.

Secondly, in these encounters, Jesus shows himself to be impatient with taboos which speak more of exclusion than embrace. Lepers, demoniacs and women ostracised as unclean evoke in him a response which ran plain counter to the conventions of his time. In the story of the woman taken in adultery (John 8:1-11) Jesus first draws the circle of sinfulness to include those who thought themselves pure, and then draws the circle of acceptance to include she who was believed to be morally beyond the pale. It is this bias towards acceptance, inclusion and embrace which is acted out again and again in Mark's sequence of encounter stories, and we must always ask ourselves what this means for us as we seek to be Christ-like people in the treatment of marginalised and vulnerable minorities in Church and society today . . . which brings us back to Mark 5:21-43.

[If you are studying this passage with other people, either divide into pairs or into two groups. One partner/ sub-group concentrates on verses 21-24 and 35-43, and the other on verses 25-34 in order to address the following questions:]

1. In relation to the sick person in your story, what happened twelve years ago?

2. Who takes the initiative in this encounter, and how would you describe the manner of their approach?

3. How did Jesus respond to being encountered in this way?

4. Fear features in your story, but why was the character in question afraid?

5. What did Jesus identify as crucial to fulfilling their hopes?

Invite partners/sub-groups to share their findings with their counterparts.

[If you are on a personal journey through this course, then take each story in turn, pose the questions in each case, and reflect on your findings.]

Some thoughts in response to these questions:

1. Twelve years is a significant period of time for both main characters, and what happened twelve years ago marks out the difference between them. The young girl was being born into a wealthy and influential family as the daughter of a synagogue president, and an anonymous woman was stricken for the first time with a distressing and socially divisive condition.

2. Jairus approaches Jesus in full view of everyone, and in spite of his status he falls to his knees and pleads with Jesus – it is a confident but humble approach. The woman with haemorrhages seeks to remain in the shadows and only diffidently and desperately reaches out to touch the hem of Jesus' robe.

3. In both cases, Jesus' power to heal is at their disposal, but in the case of Jairus he actively intervenes on behalf of his daughter, whilst in relation to the woman his power goes

from him, as it were, passively. In each case he counters their fear with an emphasis on faith.

4. Jairus is afraid because he hears that his daughter has died. The woman is afraid because she is challenged to make herself known to Jesus. In a way, Jairus is full of fear because a healing hasn't happened – and the woman because it has! But, as we shall see, there may be more to her fear than simply being found out.

5. In both cases, faith is the key.

The story of the raising of Jairus' daughter takes us on an emotional roller coaster in just a few verses. Verses 21-24 speak of desperation, and hope hanging on one last thread – perhaps Jesus can do something to make things better for this family so used to things going well. Then verses 35-43 plunge them into the depths of grief – it is too late, she is dead. But isn't this the same Jesus who said that with God all things are possible? It is all about faith which he urges on the girl's father before proceeding to rid the room of the noisome mourners so that just he with the child's mother and father, together with Peter, James and John, are there to see her restored to life.

It is worth noting that many features associated with faith healers and wonder-workers in those days are present in the raising of Jairus' daughter. A gesture – taking her by the hand; evidence – she stands up and walks around; onlookers' reaction – complete astonishment; use of a foreign phrase indicated by Mark's inclusion of the Aramaic '*talitha koum*'. But the difference is that Jesus asks for no recompense, seeks no publicity (quite the opposite!) and asks only for faith in God as the way to wholeness/salvation (the same word is used in Greek to mean 'to heal' and 'to save').

So we progress from the depths of despair to the giddy heights of hopes fulfilled in the course of this one brief encounter.

In the midst of this emotional roller coaster, another drama unfolds. This is a very brief encounter, and if the woman had had her way it would have been briefer still. In fact, she doesn't really want to encounter Jesus at all. What she wants is to receive whatever benefit he can bring her way, and then for him to go on his way unaware of her and her condition. For twelve years she has been a wallflower on the edge of society just as now, unknown and unnamed, she appears as a wallflower on the edge of the gospel story with a walk-on part and no further part to play in the grand drama of salvation unfolding around her. Or maybe the exact opposite is the case! Maybe here we have a most extraordinary prefiguring of Good Friday in this briefest of brief encounters.

Look up Leviticus 15:25-27. These verses form part of the purity laws enjoined upon the people of Israel as they became established in the Promised Land. They are strange to us, even offensive, but they would have mattered to this woman in reaching out to touch Jesus for he would thereby become himself unclean according to the terms of Levitical Law. No wonder she was afraid when he called for the person who touched his robe to come forward. He had taken her uncleanness upon himself so that she might be made clean. So she was in no way distanced from the drama of salvation. Quite the contrary, for at the heart of the Christian faith is a conviction that Jesus took to himself upon the cross all that stands between us and wholeness of life – and by faith we can claim the benefits of his Passion.

By the way

Note that this woman, coming to Jesus with very mixed motives including anger at the doctors who had failed her, desperation and even superstition, was able to tap into Jesus' healing love and power because he had a robe with a generous hem which reached beyond the crowd pressing around him. So often our churches draw their garment tightly about them to ensure purity of membership, doctrine and moral character. **[We can ask ourselves what our own church might need to do to ensure it has a generous hem which can be touched by those needing to feel the benefit of our Lord's healing presence, but who may not yet be ready to commit to what, by way of shorthand, is called organised religion.]**

For the rucksack

What from this stage of our journey will you especially want to take with you as we journey on?

Incremental prayer

Jesus Christ, Companion and Guide, go with us on this journey into life;
help us to sit loose to this world's trappings and temptations, and to travel light.
Thank you for those who have gone before us, those who go with us, and those we will encounter on the way. In meeting with us may they meet with you.

Make us unafraid to face troubled waters knowing you are our still centre at the height of the storm.

Strengthen our faith to trust in you even as the winds and waves threaten to overwhelm us – for you are the Lord of sea and sky.

Thank you for those we meet as we journey through life; make us open to what they have to teach us, show us and share with us; and may we be channels of your healing and peace to them.

Grant to us and your whole Church a generous hem to the garment of grace in which you enfold us day by day.

Amen.

Stage four
Food for the journey – food for thought
(Mark 6:30-44; 8:1-9)

Opening prayers

Blessed Lord, you have caused all holy scriptures to be written for our learning: grant that we may so hear them, read, mark, learn, and inwardly digest them, that by patience and comfort of your holy Word, we may embrace and ever hold fast the blessed hope of everlasting life, which you have given us in our Saviour Jesus Christ. Amen.

God our creator, redeemer and sustainer of life, thank you for the abundance of your provision to meet our daily needs. May justice and generosity prevail in the sharing of your bounty, especially with those in greatest need.
As we break open your Word, so may our eyes and minds be opened to all you have to teach us, that we may know more nearly, and love more dearly, your Son, Jesus Christ, our Lord. Amen.

Our Father . . .

Setting the scene

To set the scene for this stage of our journey you might be able to download some images of food, famine, picnics and shared meals via your web-search facility. A four or five minute sequence accompanied by appropriate music, will help to create atmosphere and assist meditation.

Bible reading
Mark 6:30-44

[30]The apostles gathered round Jesus and reported to him all they had done and taught. [31]Then, because so many people were coming and going that they did not even have a chance to eat, he said to them, 'Come with me by yourselves to a quiet place and get some rest.'

[32]So they went away by themselves in a boat to a solitary place. [33]But many who saw them leaving recognised them and ran on foot from all the towns and got there ahead of them. [34]When Jesus landed and saw a large crowd, he had compassion on them, because they were like sheep without a shepherd. So he began teaching them many things.

[35]By this time it was late in the day, so his disciples came to him. 'This is a remote place,' they said, 'and it's already very late. [36]Send the people away so they can go to the surrounding countryside and villages and buy themselves something to eat.'

[37]But he answered, 'You give them something to eat.'

They said to him, 'That would take eight months of a man's wages! Are we to go and spend that much on bread and give it to them to eat?'

[38]'How many loaves do you have?' he asked. 'Go and see.'

When they found out, they said, 'Five – and two fish.'

[39]Then Jesus directed them to have all the people sit down in groups on the green grass. [40]So they sat down in groups of hundreds and fifties. [41]Taking the five loaves and the two fish and looking up to heaven, he gave thanks and broke the loaves. Then he gave them to his disciples to set before

the people. He also divided the two fish among them all. [42]They all ate and were satisfied, [43]and the disciples picked up twelve basketfuls of broken pieces of bread and fish. [44]The number of the men who had eaten was five thousand.

Mark's is a short gospel and he probably had to ration the material available to him. So why include two miraculous feedings – this one, and another at chapter 8, verses 1-9?

Although they differ from one another in some respects – and you might like to have a go at spotting the differences e.g. the size of the crowd, the number of loaves and fishes, the number of baskets-full left over – the overall impression is of two stories which are essentially the same, even if the second happened 'on another occasion' (8:1).

[Why might Mark have included two such similar stories? Maybe he didn't mean to, and it was simply an oversight. This is very doubtful. Perhaps it was because such a remarkably public miracle involving so many people gains even more significance when performed a second time. In the early days of the Church this miracle would acquire powerful eucharistic overtones (breaking bread together) and so might bear repetition just as the Eucharist is celebrated over and over again.]

There has been some speculation that the first feeding represents the giving of the Bread of Life to the Jews and the second represents giving it to the Gentiles. It is pointed out that the setting of the feeding of the five thousand is Galilean i.e. Jewish territory, whilst the feeding of the four thousand is on the other side of the lake i.e. Gentile territory. The five thousand receive five loaves which possibly stand for the five books of the Mosaic Law, whilst the Gentile world was traditionally divided up into seventy nations, hence seven loaves for them. Likewise, the Gentile four thousand have seven baskets left over, whilst after the Jews are fed there are twelve baskets-full remaining as a reference to the twelve Tribes of Israel. We may even note that the Greek word for 'basket' in the five thousand story (6:43) indicates a distinctively Jewish type of basket, whilst in the four thousand account the word for 'basket' indicates an ordinary everyday fish-basket such as Gentiles might use.* This is highly speculative, but it is not implausible and it would certainly throw some light on Jesus' challenging encounter with the Syro-Phoenician woman (see below).

Clearly, Mark sees the potential of feeding stories as narrative pegs on which to hang some important teaching about discipleship and the importance of being fed spiritually as well as physically on our faith journey. Let us explore this possibility.

First of all, take a look at what follows the first feeding story. In verses 45-52 of chapter 6 we find Jesus with his disciples on the Lake of Galilee, far from the excited crowds. They see him walk on water and are utterly astounded 'for they had not understood about the loaves; their hearts were hardened' (verse 52). Next, Jesus chides the Pharisees for their failure to understand what God requires of them because they are so obsessed with their own petty rules and regulations (7:1-13). Jesus then extends his challenge to 'the people' (7:14-16) when it comes to what does and doesn't defile people in the sight of God – and soon discovers when he is alone again with the disciples that even they don't

---

* Alan Richardson, *The Miracle Stories of the Gospels* (London, 1941), p. 98.

understand what he is talking about, and he has to spell it out to them (7:17-23). To press home his point about the disciples' failure to get the message, Mark describes how a Gentile woman proves to be more perceptive and is rewarded with the healing of her mentally troubled daughter (7:24-30).

This section concludes with the curing of a man who was deaf and had an impediment in his speech (7:31-37).

By the way

Let us take a closer look at the strange and quite disturbing story of Jesus' encounter with the Syro-Phoenician woman. It clearly links with the previous section because, as a Gentile, the woman stands outside Jewish purity, and her daughter has a spirit which is 'unclean'. As in earlier encounters, she is someone who has heard about Jesus and is prepared to bow before him and beg him to cast the demon out. His response is dismissive to the point of rudeness: 'Let the children (i.e. the Jews) be fed first, for it is not right to take the children's bread and throw it to the dogs (i.e. the Gentiles)'. Whilst on the face of it she accepts the description of herself and her people as 'dogs' she is careful to make that mean dogs who are sufficiently domesticated to belong in the house and so are the beneficiaries of scraps which fall from the table. Jesus had referred to dogs that have bread thrown to them, so presumably those dogs live outside the house. The woman stakes a claim to belong to God's 'house' along with the Jews – albeit in a subordinate place. Jesus confirms his general attitude to issues of purity and uncleanness. He doesn't deny the status accorded to Jews as God's chosen people, but neither does he deny a place in God's house to those whom fastidious religious leaders believed to be beyond the pale. He accepts her rejoinder (rebuke?) and tells her that her daughter is now well. Once again, Mark uses a salutary tale to press home a point.*

Returning to the feeding miracles, the second one is recounted at the beginning of chapter 8 (verses 1-10) and once again we examine what follows from that miracle. The Pharisees come in for yet more criticism (8:11-13) but so do the disciples as they cross the lake with Jesus to the farther shore and bemoan their lack of bread (verses 14-16). 'Why are you talking about having no bread?' he asks them, 'have you no inkling yet? Do you still not understand? Are your minds closed?' He reminds them of the two feeding miracles and with mounting irritation asks them once again: 'Do you still not understand?' (verses 17-21).

This section then concludes with the restoration of a blind man's sight (verses 22-26).

[Reflect on what these sequels to the feeding stories have in common.]

Clearly much is made of failure to understand the significance of the miraculous feedings, particularly on the part of the disciples whose 'minds were closed' (6:52 and 8:17). But closed to what? What is it they didn't grasp about the miraculous feedings? Well, essentially, they should have been reminded of the miraculous provision of manna for the people of Israel in the wilderness (see Exodus 16 and Numbers 11). That was clearly God's work, and so just as stilling the storm echoed God's mastery of the elements to such an extent that they really should have recognised Jesus'

---

* David Catchpole, *Jesus People* (DLT, 2006), pp. 173-178.

divinity rather than asking 'Who is this?'(4:41), so the miraculous feedings should have enabled them to discern his true identity as Son of God.

But that is not all. Jesus' actions in relation to the feedings are typically those of a host presiding over a meal for his guests. The Jews looked forward to God presiding at a Messianic banquet for his chosen people. So the disciples might have been expected to make the connection not only with God's past provision for his people, but also with God's presidency at the final great Messianic feast. Jesus is the promised Messiah who is both human and divine, as evidenced by these miracles, but still they don't get it!

Then, significantly, the section which began with the feeding of the four thousand ends with the restoring of sight to a blind man just as the section beginning with the feeding of the five thousand ended with the healing of a deaf man. Mark uses these healing miracles to refer to the disciples' need for the restoration of their spiritual hearing and spiritual insight ('You have eyes: can you not see? You have ears: can you not hear?' 8:18).

So these stories of physical feeding and physical healing are in fact about our need for spiritual nourishment and spiritual understanding. As we journey through Lent we use fasting as one way to focus on spiritual rather than physical necessities. This message goes to the heart of Mark's Gospel as we journey with him even if it is feedings rather than fasting which provide the pegs on which to hang this timeless truth.

But it is not enough for people simply to admire what Jesus did or agree with what he said. It is necessary to acknowledge who Jesus is and so, finally, look at the verses which follow the curing of the blind man (8:27-38). At last

Peter's eyes and ears of faith are opened to perceive Jesus' true identity – but there is yet more for him to learn about what this means, and so we journey on.

For the rucksack

What from this stage of our journey will you especially want to take with you as we journey on?

Incremental prayer

Jesus Christ, Companion and Guide, go with us on this journey into life;
help us to sit loose to this world's trappings and temptations, and to travel light.
Thank you for those who have gone before us, those who go with us, and those we will encounter on the way. In meeting with us may they meet with you.

Make us unafraid to face troubled waters knowing you are our still centre at the height of the storm.
Strengthen our faith to trust in you even as the winds and waves threaten to overwhelm us – for you are the Lord of sea and sky.

Thank you for those we meet as we journey through life; make us open to what they have to teach us, show us and share with us; and may we be channels of your healing and peace to them.
Grant to us and your whole Church a generous hem to the garment of grace in which you enfold us day by day.

As we journey on we pray that you will give us each day our daily bread.

We thank you for the food which sustains our bodies and ask that you will also nourish us with the bread of life.

May we have eyes to see and ears to hear what you have to teach us through the sights and sounds along our path.

Amen.

Stage five
Followers of the way
(Mark 10:32-52)

Opening prayers

Blessed Lord, you have caused all holy scriptures to be written for our learning: grant that we may so hear them, read, mark, learn, and inwardly digest them, that by patience and comfort of your holy Word, we may embrace and ever hold fast the blessed hope of everlasting life, which you have given us in our Saviour Jesus Christ. Amen.

God our creator, redeemer and sustainer of life, thank you for leading us to this place and this time.
We praise you for Jesus, our guide and good companion, whose example we seek to follow on the road that leads through death to life eternal.
As we face up to the realities of costly discipleship, strengthen our resolve to serve you faithfully in the steps of Christ the Servant King. Amen.

Our Father . . .

Setting the scene

The scene for this stage can be set by some images of roads and highways. A web-search facility will offer a rich selection from which to download a dozen or so slides which, when accompanied by appropriate music, can help to create atmosphere and assist meditation.

Bible reading
Mark 10:32-52

[32]They were on their way up to Jerusalem, with Jesus leading the way, and the disciples were astonished, while those who followed were afraid. Again he took the Twelve aside and told them what was going to happen to him. [33]'We are going up to Jerusalem,' he said, 'and the Son of Man will be betrayed to the chief priests and teachers of the law. They will condemn him to death and will hand him over to the Gentiles, [34]who will mock him and spit on him, flog him and kill him. Three days later he will rise.'

[35]Then James and John, the sons of Zebedee, came to him. 'Teacher,' they said, 'we want you to do for us whatever we ask.'

[36]'What do you want me to do for you?' he asked.

[37]They replied, 'Let one of us sit at your right and the other at your left in your glory.'

[38]'You don't know what you are asking,' Jesus said. 'Can you drink the cup I drink or be baptised with the baptism I am baptised with?'

[39]'We can,' they answered.

Jesus said to them, 'You will drink the cup I drink and be baptised with the baptism I am baptised with, [40]but to sit at my right or left is not for me to grant. These places belong to those for whom they have been prepared.'

[41]When the ten heard about this, they became indignant with James and John. [42]Jesus called them together and said, 'You know that those who are regarded as rulers of the Gentiles lord it over them, and their high officials exercise authority over them. [43]Not so with you. Instead, whoever

wants to become great among you must be your servant, ⁴⁴and whoever wants to be first must be slave of all. ⁴⁵For even the Son of Man did not come to be served, but to serve, and to give his life as a ransom for many.'

⁴⁶Then they came to Jericho. As Jesus and his disciples, together with a large crowd, were leaving the city, a blind man, Bartimaeus (that is, the Son of Timaeus), was sitting by the roadside begging. ⁴⁷When he heard that it was Jesus of Nazareth, he began to shout, 'Jesus, Son of David, have mercy on me!'

⁴⁸Many rebuked him and told him to be quiet, but he shouted all the more, 'Son of David, have mercy on me!'

⁴⁹Jesus stopped and said, 'Call him.'

So they called to the blind man, 'Cheer up! On your feet! He's calling you.' ⁵⁰Throwing his cloak aside, he jumped to his feet and came to Jesus.

⁵¹'What do you want me to do for you?' Jesus asked him.

The blind man said, 'Rabbi, I want to see.'

⁵²'Go,' said Jesus, 'your faith has healed you.' Immediately he received his sight and followed Jesus along the road.

This passage opens with the first indication that the journey being undertaken by Jesus and his disciples leads to Jerusalem. This is a place of hostility and rejection when compared to Galilee, whose people at least gave him a hearing. Significantly, after the final confrontation in Jerusalem, it is to Galilee that Jesus returns after the resurrection (16:7).

On the way, Jesus again predicts his death. He has already forewarned the disciples of what is to befall him (see 8:31

and 9:31) and on those occasions they refused to accept what he is telling them. This time they don't argue. Perhaps the penny has dropped at last. But that doesn't prevent another side of their frail humanity kicking in so that James and John make a pitch for special favours. Jesus challenges those two about their willingness to undergo what he is facing, and when the other ten join in rebuking James and John they, too, are given a lesson in the virtues and values of the kingdom of God which are so different from those which govern those who govern in this world's corridor of power. The passage ends with another account of a healing of a blind man who then, like the disciples who have had their eyes opened to the future awaiting them, 'followed Jesus along the road' (verse 52).

By the way

Before looking more closely at what this journey of faith has to tell us about our own journey of faith and discipleship, we need to point out a few markers along the way:

- Verses 33-4: Someone once said that these verses read like 'the printed programme of a passion play' and it certainly summarises the events Mark will begin to describe in the next chapter. Like a trailer for a film, or TV documentary which shows us highlights in order to entice us to watch the programme in full, so Mark has Jesus setting out the key events about to unfold – and draws us into the drama.

- Verse 35: Note that in Matthew's version of this incident, it is their mother who enters a plea on behalf of James and John (Matthew 20:20-21). This is a nice touch and does at least partially spare the reputations of two leading figures in the early Church, but Mark's account is probably more to be trusted at this point.

- Verse 38: Here the word 'baptism' needs to be interpreted in terms of challenge and tribulation (as in our use of the phrase 'baptism of fire') rather than linking it too closely with baptism as a rite of Christian initiation. However, the fact that the reference to baptism appears alongside Jesus' reference to 'the cup that I drink' does invite us to recall the two main sacraments of the Church and the need for those who receive them to count the cost and not to treat them lightly.

[This raises issues about the terms on which baptism and Holy Communion are offered in our Churches – perhaps not a discussion to be had now, but the relevance of this verse to such a discussion needs to be noted.]

- Verse 42: The word Mark uses for 'lord it over' does not appear anywhere else in the New Testament or in classical Greek writings. So he coined it himself. He had to because top-down lording it over people was the only type of government anyone knew and they didn't need a word to describe it – it was taken for granted. This makes Jesus' prospectus for a totally different and service-centred style of leadership and authority all the more remarkable. The biblical scholar Hans-Ruedi Weber notes this radical inversion of accepted modes of authoritarianism and concludes that 'into a sick society Jesus inserts a cell of healing'.*

---

* *Experiments with Bible Study* (WCC, 1981), p.179.

[How can communities and congregations of Christians be 'cells of healing' in our society today?]

- Verse 47: There is a wonderful irony in the fact that the man who cannot see sees who Jesus is (Son of David) whilst for so long the disciples who can see don't see it at all!
- Verse 49: Note that Jesus uses other people to do the calling, and he still does – US!

Now we can take this passage in the round and see what it has to teach us as we journey on through Lent to Easter. It sees the band of followers leaving Galilee to make their way to Jerusalem via Jericho (some fifteen miles away) and on to the outskirts of the city which Jesus will enter at the beginning of the next chapter. So this is effectively the final section of Mark's extended introduction to the Passion narrative which will take a third of the gospel to cover just eight days.

Peter's recognition of Jesus as the Messiah at Caesarea Philippi (8:27-33) is the fulcrum point upon which Mark's Gospel turns. Up until then Jesus has walked, talked, healed and attracted large crowds with his miracles. But a culture of secrecy surrounds him when it comes to his true identity. Now the secret is out and the way ahead is straight to Jerusalem and all that lies in store for him there as yet another wannabe Messiah challenging the authorities and disturbing the peace. This will not be a cakewalk, and from here on in Jesus is at pains to alert the disciples to the cost and consequences of walking with him the way of the cross.

This section (10:32-52) begins and ends with Jesus and the disciples 'on the road'. The Greek word for 'road' is the same one as the Bible uses for e.g. 'the way of the Lord', and in the Acts of the Apostles Christianity itself is consistently described as 'the Way' (9:2; 19:9, 23; 22:4; 24:14, 22) just as Jesus was described by John as 'the way, the truth and the life' (John 14:6). So the exchanges which take place between Jesus and the disciples 'on the road' take on added significance because they point beyond themselves to the challenges which face all of those who seek to be followers of the Way.

[Reflect for a moment on the kind of conversations you have had on journeys. They are usually mundane and light-hearted, but very often they can be quite serious and profound – whether with friends and family or with complete strangers. Why do you think such serious conversations happen 'on the way'?]

Importantly, Jesus is 'leading the way' (verse 32). Palestinian shepherds typically led their sheep to pasture, defending them, caring for them and knowing them each by name. Jesus, the Good Shepherd, is upfront on the road to Jerusalem and it remains the case that wherever we journey as Christians our Lord leads us. This offers us reassurance, especially in times of danger and distress, but it also keeps us facing forward, drawing us on to new challenges and opportunities. As the poet R. S. Thomas put it: 'Our God is a fast God, always there before us' . . . and just as well because 'those who followed behind were afraid'. This is just the moment when we might expect a Good Shepherd to offer them words of reassurance and comfort. But no; he is confident that they can bear to hear the truth, and he won't hide the truth from them.

We like the idea of a gentle Jesus healing our hurts and massaging our fragile sense of well-being. But that is only part of the story, and when the way ahead is rough it is only right that we should be confronted honestly with that reality, rather than seek to escape into a fantasy. 'When the going gets tough' so the saying goes, 'the tough get going!'

Jesus is brutally honest with his disciples about what lies ahead of him and, by imputation, what lies ahead of them as well (verses 33 and 34).

In the middle of Lent, many of our churches are stripped bare of ornament, our hymns are dirgeful and our scripture readings are full of sober and sombre warnings. Thus we capture something of the mood which marked this small band of travellers 'on the road'. But even in the middle of Lent we take time out to enjoy some light relief on what we call Mothering Sunday or, more accurately, Refreshment Sunday. And that is right because, of course, Jesus not only told the truth about his arrest and trial, flagellation and death, he also foretold what would happen three days afterwards when 'he will rise again' (verse 34).

[Reflect on your own experience, or accounts you have heard, of a light still seeming to shine in the darkest places and the darkest times of our lives. The Light of Christ which we hail on Easter night is that light which never dies even when we are hanging on to hope only by our fingertips. Shakespeare put it this way in *The Merchant of Venice*:

How far that little candle throws his beams!
So shines a good deed in a naughty world.
(Act V scene 1)

Deeds come no better than Christ's victory over death, and its light illuminates even the darkest paths we are called to tread.]

Of course, as we have seen, the disciples were not paragons of virtue when it came to grasping the point, even when Jesus spoke to them as directly as this. James and John had been with Jesus at the Transfiguration (9:2-8) but in spite of that, or perhaps because of it, they seek to get their situation sorted when it came to the pecking order amongst his followers. Their sights have been set way beyond the messy business of betrayal, beatings and bereavement. They have their eyes on the ultimate climax to the cosmic drama, and they want the best seats in the house.

Jesus brings them down to earth sharpish. They will be called upon to share his suffering but that will be no guarantee of consequential compensation in the world to come. Service must never be self-serving, just as giving must never be another form of purchasing. Jesus came not to be served but to serve, and so it must be for us so that service is always an end in itself.

[Reflect on what that might mean for Church and Society in a culture where volunteers for charities and good causes are routinely described as unsung heroes and feature in honours lists. Perhaps we can sympathise with Frank Muir's observation that few things feel better than to do a good turn in secret and have it discovered by accident!]

Not for the first time, Mark concludes a key section of his Gospel with an account of a blind man receiving back his sight. We now know that this restoring of sight is spiritual as well as physical, and only when we have the vision to see who Jesus really is, and perceive his purpose for our lives, will we be able to join the man born blind and follow him 'on the road'.

For the rucksack

What from this stage of our journey will you especially want to take with you as we journey on?

Incremental prayer

Jesus Christ, Companion and Guide, go with us on this journey into life;
help us to sit loose to this world's trappings and temptations, and to travel light.
Thank you for those who have gone before us, those who go with us, and those we will encounter on the way. In meeting with us may they meet with you.

Make us unafraid to face troubled waters knowing you are our still centre at the height of the storm.
Strengthen our faith to trust in you even as the winds and waves threaten to overwhelm us – for you are the Lord of sea and sky.

Thank you for those we meet as we journey through life; make us open to what they have to teach us, show us and share with us; and may we be channels of your healing and peace to them.
Grant to us and your whole Church a generous hem to the garment of grace in which you enfold us day by day.

As we journey on we pray that you will give us each day our daily bread.
We thank you for the food which sustains our bodies and ask that you will also nourish us with the bread of life.
May we have eyes to see and ears to hear what you have to teach us through the sights and sounds along our path.

As followers of the way, the truth and the life,
keep our eyes fixed on you as you lead us through the valley of the shadow of death to the bright dawn of Easter Day.
Bind us body and soul to you whose service is perfect freedom, and whose way is the way that leads to life eternal.
Amen.

Cross country – Gethsemane to Golgotha

(Mark 14:32-42; 15:21-38)

Opening prayers

Blessed Lord, you have caused all holy scriptures to be written for our learning: grant that we may so hear them, read, mark, learn, and inwardly digest them, that by patience and comfort of your holy Word, we may embrace and ever hold fast the blessed hope of everlasting life, which you have given us in our Saviour Jesus Christ. Amen.

God our creator, redeemer and sustainer of life, thank you for the journey which has brought us with Jesus to Jerusalem. Now we pray that you will help us to go with him the extra mile that leads from Gethsemane to Golgotha and the Garden Tomb.
May we understand more clearly the progress and purpose of his Passion, and find at the foot of the cross a love that will not let us go.
This we ask for his dear name's sake. Amen.

Our Father . . .

Setting the scene

There are many images of the Passion and death of Jesus which can be downloaded from the internet. A sequence of them, perhaps accompanied by e.g. 'God so loved the world' from Stainer's *Crucifixion* will help to create atmosphere and assist meditation.

Bible readings
Mark 14:32-42

[32]They went to a place called Gethsemane, and Jesus said to his disciples, 'Sit here while I pray.' [33]He took Peter, James and John along with him, and he began to be deeply distressed and troubled. [34]'My soul is overwhelmed with sorrow to the point of death,' he said to them. 'Stay here and keep watch.'

[35]Going a little farther, he fell to the ground and prayed that if possible the hour might pass from him. [36]'*Abba*, Father,' he said, 'everything is possible for you. Take this cup from me. Yet not what I will, but what you will.'

[37]Then he returned to his disciples and found them sleeping. 'Simon,' he said to Peter, 'are you asleep? Could you not keep watch for one hour? [38]Watch and pray so that you will not fall into temptation. The spirit is willing, but the body is weak.'

[39]Once more he went away and prayed the same thing. [40]When he came back, he again found them sleeping, because their eyes were heavy. They did not know what to say to him.

[41]Returning the third time, he said to them, 'Are you still sleeping and resting? Enough! The hour has come. Look, the Son of Man is betrayed into the hands of sinners. [42]Rise! Let us go! Here comes my betrayer!'

Mark 15:21-39

[21]A certain man from Cyrene, Simon, the father of Alexander and Rufus, was passing by on his way in from the country, and they forced him to carry the cross. [22]They brought Jesus to the place called Golgotha (which means The Place of the

Skull). ²³Then they offered him wine mixed with myrrh, but he did not take it. ²⁴And they crucified him. Dividing up his clothes, they cast lots to see what each would get.

²⁵It was the third hour when they crucified him. ²⁶The written notice of the charge against him read: THE KING OF THE JEWS. ²⁷They crucified two robbers with him, one on his right and one on his left. ²⁹Those who passed by hurled insults at him, shaking their heads and saying, 'So! You who are going to destroy the temple and build it in three days, ³⁰come down from the cross and save yourself!'

³¹In the same way the chief priests and the teachers of the law mocked him among themselves. 'He saved others,' they said, 'but he can't save himself! ³²Let this Christ, this King of Israel, come down now from the cross, that we may see and believe.' Those crucified with him also heaped insults on him.

³³At the sixth hour darkness came over the whole land until the ninth hour. ³⁴And at the ninth hour Jesus cried out in a loud voice, *'Eloi, Eloi, lama sabachthani?'*—which means, 'My God, my God, why have you forsaken me?'

³⁵When some of those standing near heard this, they said, 'Listen, he's calling Elijah.'

³⁶One man ran, filled a sponge with wine vinegar, put it on a stick, and offered it to Jesus to drink. 'Now leave him alone. Let's see if Elijah comes to take him down,' he said.

³⁷With a loud cry, Jesus breathed his last.

³⁸The curtain of the temple was torn in two from top to bottom. ³⁹And when the centurion, who stood there in front of Jesus, heard his cry and saw how he died, he said, 'Surely this man was the Son of God!'

In Jerusalem today we can see little of the city as Jesus saw it, but the lie of the land remains the same with the Kidron Valley between the old city and the Mount of Olives, and the Temple Mount with the ancient Roman fortifications still in evidence. But just as significant as the physical remains are the sounds and smells of the Holy City which may not have changed much over the centuries, together with the radio-active religious atmosphere which seeps out from the ground beneath our feet and the walls which surround us. The city may have been fought over, bled over, built over and made over many times but it remains the city Jesus wept over – and the city which determined his destination and decided his destiny.

With his disciples Jesus headed south cross-country to Jerusalem. On the way he continued to prepare them for journey's end, and on entering the city to cries of 'Hosanna' he challenged the cult and culture of the Temple with the religious leaders on the receiving end of harsh rebukes and stern warnings (Mark 11 and 12). But it is when he is alone with his disciples that he speaks frankly about what the future holds, yes, on a cosmic scale, but also for them as his followers. The apocalyptic predictions in chapter 13 conclude with 'What I say to you, I say to everyone: Watch!'(verse 36). The journey cross-country to Jerusalem has ended, and the journey to the cross is about to begin.

Chapters 14 and 15 contain Mark's Passion narrative. Perhaps this account of Jesus' last days was already in circulation, at least in outline. It is remarkable how all four Gospels follow the same sequence of events, even if they each have their own distinctive way of telling the story. So, for example, Matthew's includes an account of the death of Judas (Matthew 27:3-10), Luke describes how Jesus was sent to see Herod (Luke 23:6-16) and John expands greatly on Jesus' trial before Pilate (John 18:28–19:16). They also put their own emphases on certain parts of the story. So Luke goes easier on the disciples, Matthew majors on miraculous happenings and John ensures that Jesus is never other than totally in control of events.

[Reflect on your own experience of accounts differing in relation to the same event – the readiness of the early Christians to tolerate or even encourage variable versions underlines their confidence in the veracity and reliability of the events themselves.]

The overall theological message of all four Passion narratives is essentially the same – and in itself it involves a journey. It is a circular journey, and it takes us to the heart of what is meant by the word *atonement.*

In the beginning it was God's will that we should live at one with God and with one another. Tragically, in the course of time, we have come to be at odds with each other and with our Maker, so that someone has to be at pains to enable us to be at one again.

At one – at odds – at pains – at one, this is the cycle of salvation which achieves at-one-ment, and it is this journey which Jesus takes from Gethsemane to Golgotha.

[Discuss members' experience of someone being at pains to secure reconciliation – the price paid for peace.]

So as Mark's Passion narrative gets underway, there is at-one-ness. Following the supper in the upper room and the walk across the Kidron Valley to the Mount of Olives and the Garden of Gethsemane, there is a strong sense of togetherness – first between Jesus and the eleven who follow him, and then between Jesus and the inner circle of Peter, James and John (14:32-42). But their solidarity with him can't survive their tiredness. They sleep, in spite of Jesus' repeated attempts to rouse them. As we have noticed, at chapter 13 verse 35, they were enjoined to 'stay awake', but now they sleep and he is alone.

By the way

In the account of the events in Gethsemane some points of interest include:

- Verse 33: The root meaning of the word translated 'troubled' is 'separated from others'. This underlines Mark's emphasis on how isolated Jesus became as the Passion narrative unfolds.

- Verse 36: The invocation 'Abba, Father' hints at the opening of the Lord's Prayer and this is reinforced by the reference in verse 38 to not being led into temptation.

- Verse 39: In Luke's narrative, there is only one occasion on which the disciples are found sleeping – this accords with his general inclination to be kinder to them. Luke's more sympathetic tendency is also evident in the sending of an angel in response to Jesus' prayer – in Mark and Matthew the response is at best ambiguous.

  We describe this episode as 'The agony in the garden'. The word agonia in Greek refers to the nervous tension experienced by an athlete before a big event.

So for Mark, Jesus' sense of isolation holds the key to how he is 'at pains' on our behalf. He is 'at odds' with his somnolent disciples, betrayed by Judas, denied by Peter and deserted by them all as he faces trial, degradation and death all alone. At last he is overwhelmed by a sense that even God has abandoned him (15:34).

In this respect Mark differs from Luke and John. Can you recall each of the seven sayings of Jesus from the cross? We may recall them, but we do not always find it easy to remember which sayings occur in which Gospel. Mark has just the one saying (15:34), and Matthew follows him (27:46). But Luke and John have three sayings each (Luke: 23:34, 43, 46; John 19:26-28, 30). In Luke they are prayerful and pastoral, whilst in John they convey a sense of Jesus always being in control. So if Mark's Jesus on the cross is clearly identifying with us in our frail and vulnerable humanity, Luke's Jesus is reaching out to us in prayer and pastoral concern whilst John's Jesus confirms that even there he is King of kings and Lord of lords, organising the family, fulfilling Scripture and declaring final victory: It is finished! At different times and in varying circumstances each of these portrayals of Jesus is precious to us. How blessed we are that in his death, as in his life, Jesus is who he needs to be in order to meet our needs, and who he longs to be in order to fulfil our longings!

Mark doesn't dwell on Jesus' physical suffering, but he does emphasise the psychological pain of being alone. At the beginning of our journey through Lent we majored on setting out with others – but now he walks alone.

[Discuss the pain of being alone in a situation of danger or distress – this is a sensitive subject and may need to be

handled with care. But there is something reassuring about Mark's recognition of aloneness as crucial to how Jesus was at pains for us by experiencing what we experience when we feel ourselves to be alone – and it is a challenge to us to be sensitive to other people's sense of isolation in a busy but sometimes careless world.]

At one, at odds, at pains: How Jesus being 'at pains' restored at-one-ness to our relationships with God and one another has been described in all sorts of ways beginning with biblical ideas of ransom, propitiation, ritual and sacrifice through to more modern images of solidarity and self-giving. The doctrine of Atonement is one doctrine which the Church has not tried to nail once and for all. Perhaps it is something we only really understand when we experience it, just as in our relationships with one another there is a sense of relief and joy when we are reconciled with someone which cannot be described but only felt with thankfulness. One thing is for sure, the resurrection of Jesus put the seal on his disciples' sense of being at one again with him and one another – but more of that next time.

Meanwhile, notice how on his journey from Gethsemane to Golgotha Jesus travelled light. He sat loose to those things which we associate with the weightiness of religion. He sits loose to:

> **Power** – whereas in John's Passion narrative Jesus is always in control, in Mark he hands over control to others. Judas hands him over to the chief priests and elders (14:44); they hand him over to Pilate (15:1), he hands him over to be crucified (15:15). Jesus' power is now the power of love which is worn lightly even as the cross weighs heavily on his back.

Buildings – the journey to Jerusalem is essentially a journey to the Temple which dominated the city in every way. It is his alleged threat to the Temple which secures his conviction (14:55-59). The Temple was huge and apparently indestructible, but its days were numbered. Within thirty years – perhaps just when Mark's Gospel was being read for the first time – it was destroyed by the Romans. This was a disaster for the Jewish people, but early Christians were learning how to travel light with Jesus as their Temple (John 2:18-22), and learning from St Paul to become themselves Temples of the Holy Spirit (I Corinthians 6:19).

Synods and Sanhedrins – it was they who condemned him.

Ritual – a simple supper sufficed along with a garden wherein to pray.

This journey is not a religious ritual but a journey of faith and trust. From Gethsemane to Golgotha Jesus entrusts himself to the reality, reliability and benevolence of the living God, so that even as the first verse of Psalm 22 is on his lips, the final three verses are in his heart.

[Once again we might find ourselves reflecting on what all this has to teach us about travelling light as a Church when it comes to buildings, synods, rituals and power.]

For the rucksack

What from this stage of our journey will you especially want to take with you as we journey on?

Incremental prayer

Jesus Christ, Companion and Guide, go with us on this journey into life;
help us to sit loose to this world's trappings and temptations, and to travel light.
Thank you for those who have gone before us, those who go with us, and those we will encounter on the way. In meeting with us may they meet with you.

Make us unafraid to face troubled waters knowing you are our still centre at the height of the storm.
Strengthen our faith to trust in you even as the winds and waves threaten to overwhelm us – for you are the Lord of sea and sky.

Thank you for those we meet as we journey through life; make us open to what they have to teach us, show us and share with us; and may we be channels of your healing and peace to them.
Grant to us and your whole Church a generous hem to the garment of grace in which you enfold us day by day.

As we journey on we pray that you will give us each day our daily bread.
We thank you for the food which sustains our bodies and ask that you will also nourish us with the bread of life.
May we have eyes to see and ears to hear what you have to teach us through the sights and sounds along our path.

As followers of the way, the truth and the life,
keep our eyes fixed on you as you lead us through the valley of the shadow of death to the bright dawn of Easter Day.
Bind us body and soul to you whose service is perfect freedom, and whose way is the way that leads to life eternal.

But when the way is hard and we are at odds with one another and with you, keep our eyes firmly fixed on the cross where you were at pains for the sake of our salvation.

We thank you that through your aloneness we are never alone, and even in the hour of our death, behold, we live!

May we who bear the weight of many cares which oppress us and possessions which possess us, learn to travel light along the way which leads to life and the dawn of Easter Day.

Amen.

Journey's end?

(Mark 16:1-8)

Opening prayers

Blessed Lord, you have caused all holy scriptures to be written for our learning: grant that we may so hear them, read, mark, learn, and inwardly digest them, that by patience and comfort of your holy Word, we may embrace and ever hold fast the blessed hope of everlasting life, which you have given us in our Saviour Jesus Christ. Amen.

God our creator, redeemer and sustainer of life, thank you for walking with us even through the valley of the shadow of death.
As Jesus bore for us the pains and insults of his Passion and death, so may we share with him the way that leads to life eternal.
Open our hearts and minds to the dawn of that day when darkness and death shall have no more dominion.
This we ask in the name of Christ risen, ascended and glorified. Amen.

Our Father . . .

Setting the scene

A sequence of images portraying garden scenes, including Easter Gardens, can be downloaded. A recording of e.g. 'Morning' from Grieg's *Peer Gynt Suite* would be a good accompaniment to create an atmosphere and assist meditation.

Last time, we left Jesus on the cross having uttered that one opening *cri-de-coeur* from Psalm 22: 'My God, my God, why have you forsaken me?' (15:34). Just as we often use the first line of a popular song to stand for the whole of it, so we might think of Jesus on the cross implying all that follows in Psalm 22 by uttering its first verse. If so, then we not only notice many cross-references to the Passion story in this Psalm **[see how many you can spot]**, but we are also struck by the fact that there is a distinct change in tone from verse 22 to the end – often signalled by a change from a minor to a major key chant in places where Psalms are sung. A note of triumph is sounded and God's victory over suffering, deprivation and death is celebrated – 'He, the Lord, has done it' (Psalm 22, verse 31). But for Mark, the cross as a throne from which Christ rules over life and death is by no means a done deal.

As we come to the end of his Gospel, we in fact come to the event that began the Christian movement. An account of the resurrection of Jesus was probably the first narrative to circulate amongst early Christians: first of all by word of mouth, but written down later. The resurrection of someone from the dead prompts the question: how did he die? So the Passion narrative took shape. But if that is how he died, what kind of life did he live? The four Evangelists answer this with accounts of his ministry beginning with his baptism and then on through Galilee to Jerusalem. One further question awaits an answer – when was he born, and where, and how? Matthew and Luke supply infancy narratives to complete the picture. But not quite, because John pre-empts a further thought. If that is how he was born, lived, died and rose again, where was he before all that came to pass? 'In the beginning was the Word', John tells us, 'and the Word was with God' (John 1:1). The question of who Jesus was, especially in relation to his identity as the Son of God, gets pushed back to the very moment of creation – but, of course, the questioning began with the event with which the Gospels ended. And it is Mark's ending to the great Jesus drama which is most beguiling and mysterious.

Bible reading
Mark 16:1-8

¹When the Sabbath was over, Mary Magdalene, Mary the mother of James, and Salome bought spices so that they might go to anoint Jesus' body. ²Very early on the first day of the week, just after sunrise, they were on their way to the tomb ³and they asked each other, 'Who will roll the stone away from the entrance of the tomb?'

⁴But when they looked up, they saw that the stone, which was very large, had been rolled away. ⁵As they entered the tomb, they saw a young man dressed in a white robe sitting on the right side, and they were alarmed.

⁶'Don't be alarmed,' he said. 'You are looking for Jesus the Nazarene, who was crucified. He has risen! He is not here. See the place where they laid him. ⁷But go, tell his disciples and Peter, "He is going ahead of you into Galilee. There you will see him, just as he told you."'

⁸Trembling and bewildered, the women went out and fled from the tomb. They said nothing to anyone, because they were afraid.

It is now generally accepted that Mark's Gospel originally ended at chapter 16 verse 8: 'the women went out and fled from the tomb. They said nothing to anyone, because they were afraid.' This is a strange way to bring such an epic journey to a close, so efforts were made to provide something more. But these longer endings, still to be found in most versions of the New Testament, seem to be compiled from accounts of Jesus' resurrection appearances in the other Gospels – no such accounts occur in Mark's original.

By the way

A fascinating story lies behind our confidence that Mark's Gospel did indeed end at verse 8 of chapter 16. In 1844 Count Constantin Tischendorf spent some time at St Catherine's Monastery at the foot of what is believed to be Mount Sinai in Egypt. During his stay he was supplied with some old manuscripts for use as fuel to counter the cold nights. He quickly realised that these manuscripts were very ancient biblical texts and, by means not altogether honourable, he managed to acquire them for further study. Indeed, they turned out to comprise one of the most important manuscripts of the Greek Bible, now known as Codex Sinaiticus and dating from the early fourth century. To Tischendorf's surprise, and to the surprise of many since, this most reliable of sources has Mark's Gospel ending at chapter 16, verse 8. Codex Sinaiticus can now be seen at the British Museum.

Why might Mark have omitted any reference to Jesus appearing to the disciples in the Upper Room or by the lakeside or on the road to Emmaus? It is more than likely that such stories were in circulation by the time he came to write his Gospel so this would have been a deliberate omission on his part. Why? **[Some time spent reflecting on this question might be appropriate at this point.]**

We may never know the answer for sure, but the way Mark ends his account of events at the empty tomb suggests that he has a real feel for suspense – like the ending of the Passion narrative, he leaves us with a bit of a cliffhanger.

[Reflect here on the different musical cadences with which we are familiar. John's Gospel ends with what is called a perfect cadence to round off his Gospel in a way that is satisfyingly conclusive. The same may not be said for Matthew and Luke whose endings are more like imperfect or 'suspended' cadences whilst Mark ends with what might be described as a rather 'scary' cadence, such as might be used in film music to evoke a sense of tension and uncertainty.]

For Matthew, the resurrection represents the dramatic in-breaking of the kingdom of heaven. A decisive battle against sin and death has been fought and won, but the war goes on. We who would be followers of Christ are commissioned to go on fighting for good against evil, for right against wrong. For Matthew the resurrection is not so much an end, as the beginning – the beginning of the end. The battle cry is 'Onward Christian Soldiers', and do not rest until the new world order inaugurated by the resurrection of Jesus has become a reality for all people everywhere. What Matthew provides by way of an ending is what is called an 'interrupted' or 'suspended' cadence which leaves the listener waiting for the resolution of what is otherwise still unresolved – the end is now, but not yet.

For Luke, the resurrection is likewise a suspended cadence. The risen Jesus points the way forward for his disciples, and Luke's second volume describes the acts of the Apostles as they take forward his mission 'throughout all Judea and Samaria, and even in the farthest corners of the earth' (Acts 1:8). For Luke the resurrection is not so much the end, or the beginning of the end, but the end of the beginning. There is more work to be done and, as disciples of Christ, we are the ones to do it. We are empowered and emboldened by the resurrection to work God's will in the world because we know that never again will evil and death have the last word. For Luke, as for Matthew, the resurrection signifies unfinished business – work in progress.

However, for all the dramatic power and intensity evident in the Gospel endings crafted by John, Matthew and Luke, it is Mark's telling of the resurrection story which is the most remarkable. After the women find the tomb empty, and are told by the young man inside the tomb that Jesus has been raised, he has gone ahead of them to Galilee, and they must tell this to Peter and the other disciples, Mark simply reports that:

> the women went out and fled from the tomb. They said nothing to anyone, because they were afraid. (Mark 16:8)

Somehow, what they had seen and heard was just too hot to handle. They knew the world as it was where sin and evil held sway, and dead people stayed dead, and they had sort of learned to live with it, to accommodate it, to compromise with it. But this news of a risen Lord was overwhelming. They were not brave enough for this brave new world, and Mark leaves them and us in a state of fear and trembling. For Mark, the resurrection as the end of the Jesus story signals no end of trouble for those who dare to follow him. This is most definitely a cliffhanger of an ending for which the musical equivalent will be a very scary cadence indeed.

Francis J. Maloney describes how the women ran away from the tomb 'associating themselves with the fear, trembling, astonishment and flight of the disciples' (see Mark 14:50-52).* For Maloney, as for many other commentators, the theme of failure is key to understanding Mark's Gospel. The cross is communicated as an apparent failure of Jesus' mission which, like him, hangs there abandoned and aborted. The disciples are regularly portrayed as failing to understand his message and they prove frail and fragile in the face of dangers and temptations. It would appear that God took enormous risks in the act of Incarnation, and Jesus likewise took risks when it came to recruiting disciples and retaining them. Somehow, there is little in all of this to make us feel that it has much to do with religion which we generally experience as risk-averse, allergic to failure and routinely robust in recruiting its representatives. But it is strong on faith – faith in God's promises which are never found to fail notwithstanding the fears and failures of those called to follow him. This is why Mark is able to end his Gospel as he does. The disciples know, and Mark's readers know, that throughout his journeying with them Jesus' promises always come true and, of course, the most important of these promises related to his death and resurrection (Mark 8:31; 9:31; 10:33, 34). This being so, Mark's readers have every reason to believe that the promises found in Mark 14:28 and 16:7 about meeting the disciples in Galilee after the resurrection must have been fulfilled so that the fear which overcame the women was itself overcome by the faith which God's promises inspire. Fear and failure redeemed

---

* Francis J. Maloney, *Mark – Storyteller, Interpreter, Evangelist* (Hendrickson, 2004), p.112.

through faith is truly good news for those who first read Mark's Gospel, and remains good news for all who read Mark's Gospel today.

Perhaps we are too ready to look to religion to round things off in neat and tidy ways – including the journey we have made through Lent to Easter. Jesus promised to be with his disciples 'even to the end of time' (Matthew 28:20) and it is that promise which overcame fear with faith as the disciples came to terms with the reality of the empty tomb on Easter Day. It is that faith which we take with us as we journey on, with Mark continuing to provide a route map for followers of the Way.

For the rucksack

What from this journey will you especially want to take with you as we journey on into God's future for us?

Incremental prayer

Jesus Christ, Companion and Guide, go with us on this journey into life;
help us to sit loose to this world's trappings and temptations, and to travel light.
Thank you for those who have gone before us, those who go with us, and those we will encounter on the way. In meeting with us may they meet with you.

Make us unafraid to face troubled waters knowing you are our still centre at the height of the storm.
Strengthen our faith to trust in you even as the winds and waves threaten to overwhelm us – for you are the Lord of sea and sky.

Thank you for those we meet as we journey through life; make us open to what they have to teach us, show us and share with us; and may we be channels of your healing and peace to them.
Grant to us and your whole Church a generous hem to the garment of grace in which you enfold us day by day.

As we journey on we pray that you will give us each day our daily bread.
We thank you for the food which sustains our bodies and ask that you will also nourish us with the bread of life.
May we have eyes to see and ears to hear what you have to teach us through the sights and sounds along our path.

As followers of the way, the truth and the life,
keep our eyes fixed on you as you lead us through the valley of the shadow of death to the bright dawn of Easter Day.
Bind us body and soul to you whose service is perfect freedom, and whose way is the way that leads to life eternal.

But when the way is hard and we are at odds with one another and with you, keep our eyes firmly fixed on the cross where you were at pains for the sake of our salvation.
We thank you that through your aloneness we are never alone, and even in the hour of our death, behold, we live!
May we who bear the weight of many cares which oppress us and possessions which possess us, learn to travel light along the way which leads to life and the dawn of Easter Day.

Christ crucified for us, suffering with us and victorious even over death, we thank you for that love which reached through the pain to touch our lives with forgiveness and a share in your resurrected life.

Even through our fears and failures we know that you go before us to prepare the way we are called to follow.
Be with us when we journey together as your pilgrim people, and may your light shine brightly through our lives now and always.
Amen.